FIRST COMMUNION

A BOOK OF PREPARATION

THE REV. JAMES G. GOOLD, M.A.

THE SAINT ANDREW PRESS

CONTENTS

PASSAGES OF SCRIPTURE BEARING
UPON THE LORD'S SUPPER

I. St Matthew xxvi. 26-30

26. And as they were eating, Jesus took bread, and blessed it, and brake it, and gave it to the disciples, and said, Take, eat; this is my body. 27. And he took the cup, and gave thanks, and gave it to them, saying, Drink ye all of it; 28. For this is my blood of the new covenant, which is shed for many for the remission of sins. 29. But I say unto you, I will not drink henceforth of this fruit of the vine, until that day when I drink it new with you in my Father's kingdom. 30. And when they had sung an hymn, they went out into the mount of Olives

II. i Corinthians xi. 23-29

23. For I have received of the Lord that which also I delivered unto you, That the Lord Jesus the same night in which he was betrayed took bread : 24. And when he had given thanks, he brake it, and said, Take, eat : this is my body, which is broken for you : this do in remembrance of me. 25. After the same manner also he took the cup, when he had supped saying, This cup is the new covenant in my blood : this do ye, as oft as ye drink it, in remembrance of me. 26. For as often as ye eat this bread, and drink this cup, ye do shew the Lord's death till he come. 27. Wherefore whosoever shall eat this bread, and drink this cup of the Lord, unworthily, shall be guilty of the body and blood of the Lord. 28. But let a man examine himself, and so let him eat of that bread, and drink of that cup. 29. For he that eateth and drinketh unworthily, eateth and drinketh judgment to himself, not discerning the Lord's body.

Note.—The words " covenant " and " judgment " are used above as in the Revised Version, instead of the "testament" and "damnation" of the Authorised Version.

III. i Corinthians x. 16, 17, 21

16. The cup of blessing which we bless, is it not the communion of the blood of Christ ? The bread which we break. is it not the communion of the body of Christ ? 17. For we being many are one bread, and

one body : for we are all partakers of that one bread . . . 21. Ye cannot drink the cup of the Lord, and the cup of devils : ye cannot be partakers of the Lord's table, and of the table of devils.

IV. St John vi. 35, 56

35. And Jesus said unto them, I am the bread of life : he that cometh to me shall never hunger ; and he that believeth on me shall never thirst . . . 56. He that eateth my flesh, and drinketh my blood, dwelleth in me, and I in him.

THE SHORTER CATECHISM ON THE LORD'S SUPPER

Question 92.— What is a Sacrament ?

A Sacrament is an holy ordinance instituted by Christ ; wherein, by sensible signs (*i.e.* signs that appeal to the senses of touch, sight, etc.), Christ, and the benefits of the new covenant, are represented, sealed (confirmed), and applied to believers.

Question 96.—What is the Lord's Supper ?

The Lord's Supper is a Sacrament, wherein, by giving and receiving bread and wine, according to Christ's appointment, His death is shewed forth ; and the worthy receivers are, not after a corporal and carnal manner, but by faith, made partakers of His body and blood, with all His benefits, to their spiritual nourishment and growth in grace.

Question 97.—What is required to the worthy receiving of the Lord's Supper ?

It is required of them that would worthily partake of the Lord's Supper, that they examine themselves of their knowledge to discern the Lord's body (*i.e.* to perceive in the sign the thing signified ; to recognise that they are not dealing only with bread and wine, but with Christ), of their faith to feed upon Him of their repentance. love, and new obedience ; lest coming unworthily, they eat and drink judgment to themselves.

CHAPTER I

BECOMING A COMMUNICANT

i. What "Joining the Church" means

YOU have come to the point at which you are thinking seriously of becoming a communicant in the Church. This is commonly known as "joining the Church," but that is an error. If you were baptised as a child you were received into the Church then, and have been a member of it ever since, though not a full member—just as you have always belonged to the country of your parents, but are not a full citizen till you reach maturity and receive the right to vote.

To become a communicant is to make the public profession that you are going to be attached to the Church henceforward, no longer from mere custom, or because your parents dedicated you to God at your baptism, but because you have taken your stand of your own free will on the side of Jesus Christ. When you can say with all your heart that you acknowledge Him as your Saviour and Master, and are determined to live your life by faith in Him, then you *ought* to come to that sacrament in which His disciples pledge themselves to Him and meet Him in loving communion.

ii. The Right Age to become a Communicant

Who can say what is the 'right' age at which to become a communicant member of the Church? To the young one could say — If you are old enough to go to work or to university or further education college, you are old enough to know the meaning of confessing Christ as your Lord. But there are also those who, for various reasons, have waited until much later before taking this important step. Whenever there is a true desire to come to communion do not put it off, for by the time you are a few years older the desire may have passed. If you are really trusting Christ and trying to be His disciple, come to His table without fear and without shame whatever your age. John Wesley was a communicant when he was eight, but for most people that would be too young.

iii. Who are Fit to be Communicants?

In the strict sense; *no one* is fit to be a communicant. Every person falls far short of what a true Christian ought to be. But we come to the Lord's table, not because we are saints, but because we are sinners, needing His forgiveness and trusting in His help. We do well to be afraid of "eating and drinking unworthily"; but we are not reckoned "unworthily" if we are *penitent* sinners, but only if we are indifferent and impenitent.

If you feel that Jesus Christ is nothing to you, if you have no desire for the life that

He can give, if you do not intend to abandon the sins from which He wishes to save you, you certainly ought not to come to communion. That would be to make a false profession. But in that case are there not some other very solemn questions that you need to ask yourself ?

If, however, you believe that Jesus is the only true Lord and Saviour of men, and that only through Him our sins are forgiven and we are enabled to live the life that is pleasing to God, and if you have resolved to trust Him as your personal Saviour and look to Him for help, you ought to come to communion and take your stand among His professed disciples. It is a mean thing to be ashamed to confess Jesus. "Whosoever shall be ashamed of Me and of My words, of him also shall the Son of Man be ashamed, when He cometh in the glory of His Father with the holy angels" (Mark viii. 38).

iv. Some Difficulties in the Way

1. *Perhaps you cannot trace the beginnings of your Christian life so clearly as you would like.*— But though some people can tell you the very day when they were converted, many a true Christian cannot. The important thing is not when or how you came to Christ, but whether you are sure you are His now.

2. *Perhaps you cannot meanwhile assent to all the doctrines of the Church, and you do not wish to be insincere.*—But the test of discipleship is not correct opinion, but devotion to

Christ. The church must, of necessity, apply certain doctrinal tests to its ministers and office-bearers, but it will welcome joyfully to the Lord's table any one who has truly taken Christ as Lord and Saviour.

3. *Perhaps you are kept back because there are some in the Church whose lives are inconsistent with their profession.*—Well, among the Twelve there was a Judas who betrayed, and a Peter who denied, and others who "forsook Him and fled"; would you, therefore, have objected to be one of the Twelve? A Church that professes to contain none but true Christians is apt soon to become a Church of hypocrites. No one can pronounce with assurance in every case who should and who should not be members of the Church. "The Lord knoweth them that are His." It is safest, except in cases of scandalous sin, to "let both grow together until the harvest." Our business is not to be judging our neighbours, but to make sure that we ourselves are true disciples.

4. *Perhaps you think you have no need of the Church,* you can do well enough without it, you can be a good enough Christian without attaching yourself to any body of Christians. —But that is not how brave men argue when the trumpet calls to war. No one says, "I can be just as good a soldier without joining the army"! Christianity is a religion of fellowship, and Christian people must unite for mutual help and common service. If

you stand aside you will not be as good a man or woman, or render as useful service to your Lord, as if you humbly take your place in the great fellowship of disciples. Can you imagine St Paul refusing to identify himself with the Church ? Neither in religion nor in life can we stand alone.

v. Some Reasons for Observing the Sacrament of the Lord's Supper

A sacrament is an act of worship appointed by Christ, in which, by the use of outward and visible signs, such as bread and wine, we proclaim deep spiritual truths, and receive the grace of the Lord Jesus Christ.

This sacrament is precious because it is so fully in accordance with human nature. It is Christ's own answer to our longing for some visible sign of His holy presence. Our souls are reached through our senses. Think how we are stirred by great pictures or noble music. The wedding ring is a constant call to love and faithfulness. The flag kindles our patriotism. The keepsakes of our beloved dead awake our tenderest memories. And here is a simple thing that the Saviour of the world asks us to do to keep us from forgetting that He died for love of us, and " ever liveth " to save. " Do this in remembrance of Me."

1. Our first and strongest reason, then, is just that *Jesus Himself asks us to " do this."* Even if we did not quite see the use of it, would it not be enough, to begin with, that

it is His wish ?   Can we not trust Him to have had sufficient reasons ?

2. But we do see the use of it.   *This observance keeps the Church always very close to Christ.*....Christianity is not merely a set of high principles; or a body of doctrine ; it is a life of remembrance of Jesus, and obedience to Him, and trust in Him.   And the Lord's Supper assuredly helps us to remember that at the heart of our religion is this personal devotion to our Saviour.

3. *It continually refreshes our love for Christ.* —He loves us, and wants us to love Him; and for hundreds of years it has been found that there is no act of worship that helps to keep our love deep and true like this remembrance of His sacrifice in the very way He has Himself appointed.

4. *It is a way by which we express our gratitude to Christ.*—If we believe that He, God's only-begotten Son, died for us ; if we ever feel, as St Paul did, " He loved me, and gave Himself for me " ; and if we know that He is our Saviour indeed and has brought us to God. and given us pardon and eternal life : we shall love to keep the memorial of His death.   The day of Calvary will be to us the most wonderful and sacred day in history.   " God forbid that I should glory, save in the cross of our Lord Jesus Christ."   We shall come to communion because we love Him and wish to show our gratitude to Him for giving us life by His death.

5. *It is a way of serving Christ.*—By doing this we add our tiny stone to the great cairn of witness. Our Lord wishes to draw the eyes of all the world to His cross; and here is something that even the least of us can do to carry out His wish : " As often as ye eat this bread and drink this cup ye do *show* (*proclaim*) the Lord's death till He come."

6. *It is a way of meeting Christ Himself, and receiving Him to dwell in our hearts.*—As we lovingly remember His example, He comes to us to be our life.

CHAPTER II

THE LORD'S SUPPER: I. HOW IT BEGAN

IT was instituted on the evening before our Lord was crucified, " the same night in which He was betrayed." Jesus loved the religious services of His people, and He had a great longing to keep the Passover with His disciples once more before He died (Luke xxii. 15). The Passover was the annual feast of thanks-giving which the Israelites had kept for hundreds of years—and all good Jews keep it still—in remembrance of God's goodness in delivering them from the Egyptian bondage. You should read again Exodus xii., especially verses 21-39, which tells the beautiful old story, and why this feast was called the Passover.

The way they celebrated it was this. When the appointed evening arrived, each family, or little group of families, or company of friends like Jesus and His disciples, gathered round the supper table. The head of the house offered a prayer of thanksgiving to God for His deliverance of His people. A cup of wine was drunk, and the company solemnly washed their hands in token of the need of purity of heart. The youngest person present then asked what this strange service meant, and a long explanation was given. The Passover lamb denoted that the Lord had *passed over, i.e.* spared, the houses of the Hebrews. The unleavened bread spoke of the haste of their departure ; they had not had time to put leaven (yeast) in the dough. The bitter herbs were a memorial of the bitterness of the Egyptian bondage.

After this explanation Psalms cxiii. and cxiv. were sung, and then the supper proper began. The head of the house took a cake of bread, and broke it, and gave thanks, and gave a piece to every one at table. Then the lamb was eaten with the bread and bitter herbs and sauce.

After supper the head of the house again took a cup of wine and gave thanks—a sort of grace after meat—from which this cup was known as " the cup of blessing." And the Passover concluded with the singing of " an hymn " (Matt. xxvi. 30), which consisted of Psalms cxv. to cxviii., Psalms of Jubilant praise, for the Passover was the nation's great festival of thanksgiving.

And that night Jesus turned it into a festival of thanksgiving of a different kind. He was at the head of the table, and He observed the usual order until He took the bread just before they ate the supper. But at that point, instead of speaking about the deliverance from Egypt, He gave a new meaning to the bread : " This is My body, broken for you. Do this in remembrance of Me." He was asking His disciples to keep the feast in remembrance, not of the deliverance from Egypt, but of the far more wonderful deliverance, the eternal salvation, bestowed on us through His sacrifice.

After supper He took " the cup of blessing," and to it also He gave a new meaning : " This is My blood of the new covenant, which is shed for many for the remission of sins."

He did not formally abolish the Passover, but the new meaning He gave to the bread and the cup so overshadowed all thoughts of the deliverance from Egypt that even His Jewish disciples soon gave up keeping the Jewish Passover, and all the Christians, Jewish and Gentile alike, kept instead our Lord's simple but moving sacrament of His body and blood.

CHAPTER III

THE LORD'S SUPPER: II. WHAT IT MEANS

i. Thanksgiving

IT is the great Christian sacrament of thanksgiving for the love that saved us. We also " take bread, and give thanks." The love of the Father in giving His only-begotten Son, the love of the Son in giving Himself to save us, the forgiveness of sins, the new life we have in Him, His presence with us " even unto

the end of the world," the hope we have of
the blessed life with Him hereafter : how can
we help giving thanks for these things, and
feeling our hearts very full of love and wonder
as the bread is broken again and the cup
received ?   It is because the Lord's Supper is
our sacrament of thanksgiving that it is
often called the " Eucharist."   (*Eucharistesas*
is the Greek for " when He had given thanks,"
1 Cor. xi. 24.)

ii. Commemoration: "This do in Remembrance of Me"

1. *It Commemorates Jesus Himself.*—We
come together not merely to eat the bread
and drink the cup and be together in the
worship of God, but to remember that it is
Jesus who brings us to God.   Jesus is Himself
the very centre and life of our religion.   We
are not to remember God and forget Jesus.
The God we worship and trust and love is
the God whom we have seen in the life and
the cross of the Man of Nazareth.

2. *It Commemorates the death of Jesus, not
just His life or words.*—You must never forget
that this is the meaning given to the sacrament
by our Lord Himself :   "This is My body
broken for you—My blood *shed* for many for
the remission of sins."   Some people say that
the Church has laid too much emphasis on
the death of Jesus, but it is He Himself who
asks us to lay this emphasis on it.   Does not
that show that He attached a very sacred
meaning to His death ?

At the Lord's Supper, therefore, we keep before us, by means of the Scripture passages we read and the hymns we sing, the events of that awful night and day—the betrayal, the agony in Gethsemane, the mockery and scourging, the indescribable suffering of the crucifixion. Jesus our Lord, Jesus the sinless, Jesus the only-begotten Son of God, was treated thus by the world He came to save.

3. *It commemorates not just the historical facts, but the meaning and purpose of the suffering and death of our Lord.* — We do not remember merely the wounds and the pain and death of the men who died in war ; we remember that they died *for us*, died to keep their country free. It is never the mere fact that interests us, it is the *meaning* of the fact — what we call the doctrine of it. What is the meaning of the death of Jesus?

It means that the reconciliation of the world to God was not easy. It was not accomplished by a word or a miracle, but by the supreme, loving act and agony of Almighty God, by the Son of God coming into the midst of the shame and sin and pain of humanity, and living the life that led to Calvary. Our salvation cost no less than *that."* "He suffered for our sins, the just for the unjust that He might bring us to God." God has forgiven us and reconciled us to Himself by the loving, patient, terrible way of the incarnation and the cross.

So we commemorate at the Lord's Supper, not simply the cross, but the redeeming love that was behind it. " He loved me, and gave Himself for me."

iii. Communion

1. *Communion with the Lord Jesus Christ.*

It is an act not only of commemoration of a dead Teacher, but of fellowship with a living Saviour. You go to communion to meet Jesus Christ, who is alive for evermore.

You may meet Christ at any time and in any place, and have communion with Him in prayer. But it is a peculiarly sacred and impressive act of communion when the Church comes together to meet its Lord in His own sacrament. His presence, His grace, His appeal to us, are realised there with exceptional vividness and solemnity.

So when you speak of " going to communion " you are not using a mere figure of speech ; you are really going to meet Christ and commune with Him. Communion is a contact of two personalities. At the communion you are giving your *thoughts* to Christ, to what He was and did and suffered ; you are giving your *feelings* to Christ, letting your love be warmed by the remembrance of all we owe to Him ; and you are giving your *will* to Christ, resolving to be true to Him and to make a brave fight against sin.

And what does Christ give you ? Think what a precious thing it is to be close to Him for a little while in this way and yield yourself to the influence of His Spirit. He is giving you *Himself.* He is deepening your sorrow for sin, renewing your faith, strengthening your will to a holier life, kindling that love of Himself which is the supreme inspiration to purity, and love of others, and self-denial for the right.

When Jesus set apart certain portions of bread and wine—simple things that we can eat and drink—and called them " My body " and " My blood," He was plainly teaching three things : (1) that He would continue to be personally present with His people ; (2) that they would be able to receive Him into their inmost being as the nourishment of their souls, the very bread and wine of their lives ; and (3) that whenever they observed His sacrament in faith and love they would actually obtain this infinite Gift. The great truth is nobly put in the Shorter Cate-chism (Q. 96), " the worthy receivers are, not after a corporal or carnal manner, but by faith, *made partakers of His body and blood, with all His benefits,* to their spiritual nourish-ment, and growth in grace."

So there is a " real presence " of Christ in the communion. You are dealing with the Lord Himself, not just with thoughts and mem-ories of Him. We Protestants do not believe that the bread and wine are changed literally into His body and blood ; we do believe that in the sacrament they become the means by which He draws near to those that love Him, to be the food and drink of their souls. When strips of coloured cloth are sewn together in a particular way they are no longer *merely* bits of cloth, but the country's flag, which means freedom and justice and glorious memories of courage and sacrifice. And when the bread and the cup are solemnly set apart at the table to their holy use, they are no longer *merely* bread and wine, but memorials of the Saviour, signs of His living presence, a means of loving communion with Him, and of actually receiving the blessings of His salvation. All who partake of them in humble faith do indeed receive Jesus Christ. They do not receive Him in any other way than they do in prayer, but most people meet their Lord more intimately in His holy sacrament than they do even in prayer. " We get no other thing, nor no new thing, in the sacrament, but the same thing which we get in the Word. . . . Yet thou gets that same thing better " (Robert Bruce, minister of Edinburgh, sixteenth century).

What is offered to us at the communion is therefore nothing less than Christ Himself—crucified, risen, ascended, interceding. He is offering Himself to all of us in His unspeakable love, even as in His earthly life He offered Himself to be the Friend and Saviour of all who would receive Him. He is offering Himself whether we accept Him or not. But it makes a great difference to us whether we meet His offer with utter hardness, like Judas, or with devotion and love, like John.

" THE LORD IS HERE ; LET US ADORE."

2. *Communion of the members of the Church with one another.*

The Lord's Supper has always been the supreme assertion of the brotherhood of

Christian people. Differences between rich
and poor, master and servant, educated and
uneducated, should be forgotten there. All
alike are sinful men and women, who need
the pardon and help of God. Bitterness and
pride and malice must have no place among
those who come together to hold communion
with One who died for love of them.

It is also the great witness to the real unity
of the Church. Christian people, with all
their divisions, are one in trusting Jesus Christ
as Saviour and Lord. This is *the Lord's* table ;
our Church heartily invites to it people of all
Churches, who love Him and desire to meet
Him in His sacrament ; and we pray for the
time when Christians of all denominations
may be willing to unite in the communion of
His body and blood.

3. *A pledge of the perfected communion of
heaven.*

Our Lord wishes us not only to look back
to Calvary, but look forward to the great
consummation : " I will not drink henceforth
of this fruit of the vine, until that day when
I drink it new with you in My Father's kingdom." And St Paul says, " Ye do shew the
Lord's death *till He come.*" The Lord's
Supper is the reminder that we shall all meet
Christ again, and those that are His shall be
with Him for ever. At our communion we
are, as it were, making an appointment with
Him. We are promising that we shall make
ourselves ready for Him, and not fail Him
" in that day."

iv. Consecration

Jesus said, " This cup is the new covenant in My blood." What is a covenant ? and why did He call it the *new* covenant ?

A covenant is an agreement, or compact, in which two persons make promises to one another. God has chosen Israel to be the channel of His supreme revelation to the world. " I will be your God, and ye shall be My people " (Lev. xxvi 12 ; Jer. vii, 23, etc.). This was the *old* covenant, and with long-suffering grace He had fulfilled all His promises. When God makes a covenant with His people it is always a covenant of *grace;* the love and the patience and the promise-keeping are mostly on His side.

But now Jesus says, " This cup is the *new* covenant." There is a more intimate and gracious relation henceforward, not between God and Israel alone, but between God and all who accept Jesus as their Saviour. He grants them a knowledge of Himself, and a full forgiveness of sin, and a power for righteousness, such as had never been known before. And all this has come through the sacrifice of Jesus in living and dying to reconcile men to God : " This cup is the new covenant *in My blood.*"

So when you take the cup you are entering into the new covenant. You are making a solemn promise to your Lord.

1. *What do you promise Him* ?

You promise to take Him for your Saviour,

to accept humbly the forgiveness of sins that He brings you, to obey Him and to serve Him.

Here is a covenant subscribed in the days of the Scottish Covenants by fifteen girls of Midlothian : " This is a covenant made between the Lord and us with our whole hearts, to give up ourselves freely to Him, without reserve, soul and body, to be His children, and Him to be our God and Father . . ."* That is the sort of consecration of ourselves that we should all be making at the communion, and that is why we call the Lord's Supper a sacrament of *consecration*. Those who are partaking in the right spirit are giving themselves afresh to their Lord.

We are so made that we feel a pledge to be more impressive and sacred when we make it, not only by an inward resolve, or even by word of mouth, but by some outward act, such as signing a name or putting on a wedding ring. What a sacred pledge it is to take the cup that is the symbol of Jesus' blood ! This then is the solemn act by which we continually renew our covenant with Christ.

2. *What does He promise you* ?

Just everything — all that is included in that wonderful word *salvation* — forgiveness, power to conquer sin, the gladness and peace of His companionship.

He promises a share in His sufferings too, perhaps. We have little real fellowship with Him if we have nothing in common with His spirit of loving service. Communion with

* Hewison, *The Covenanters.*

Jesus in His broken body and shed blood means willingness to share with Him the burden of the world's sorrow and sin, to do and suffer disagreeable and painful things for Him to have *our* bodies broken for His sake, and to drink the cup that He drank.

And He promises an entrance at the last into His joy. As we renew the covenant we are entitled to think of the day when, for all who are His, life shall reach its perfect fulness. "The Lamb that is in the midst of the throne shall feed them, and shall lead them unto living fountains of waters."

It is because the Lord's Supper is filled with all this sacred meaning that St Paul says, "Let a man examine himself, and *so* let him eat of this bread and drink of this cup." Make sure that you are in earnest. There is only one question, on our answer to which our eternal destiny depends. It is the simple question, How do I stand to Jesus Christ? Am I sincerely and with all my heart on His side?

Let a man examine *himself*. No minister or other friend can probe the secrets of your heart. You alone know whether you have really taken Jesus for your Saviour and Master.

CHAPTER IV
THE COMMUNION SERVICE

i. Preparation for the Communion

THE questions suggested at the close of the last chapter are to be asked, not once for all when you are first received as a communicant, but at *every* communion. Amid the coarsening influences of the world it is easy to drift away from Christ.

> " To keep your armour bright
> Attend with constant care,
> Still walking in your Captain's sight,
> And watching unto prayer."

You never go even to a party or entertainment in which you have to take a part, however small, without giving it a good deal of thought beforehand. And you cannot be feeling very deeply about Jesus if you can go to meet Him at His table without having taken any trouble to prepare your mind for what you are about to do. It is sure to deaden your religious life if you go to a service so solemn with your mind full of your work and your pleasures.

In the days before communion you should seek a few quiet moments for self-examination. Do not take it for granted that, because you *once* felt your heart glow with devotion to Jesus, all is well with you still. Such questions as the following ought to be answered truthfully to your own conscience : —

Have I really been trying to live so as to please my Lord ?

Have I been doing all I could to keep near Him ?

Have I prayed with regularity and sincerity, or have my prayers been merely formal, or have I given up real prayer altogether ?

Have I been doing anything which I know to be sinful ?

Have I tried honestly to turn my mind away from forbidden thoughts and feelings ?

Have I tried to do any definite thing for Jesus' sake ?

If you are indulging deliberately in any known sin, and have no intention of giving it up, do not go to communion. Do not eat and drink judgment to yourself. But ask yourself soberly, " What shall be the end of them that obey not the gospel of God ? " " God is not mocked."

Confess your sins and failures with sincere repentance and desire to do better ; make honourable acknowledgment and reparation for any wrong you have done. Then you may humbly and gratefully trust that God, who is " faithful and just to forgive you your sins, and to cleanse you from all unrighteousness," will receive you and renew His grace to you at His table.

Before going to communion, make an offering of yourself to Jesus in such words as these :

O Lord Jesus,

Help me to love Thee better than I have done ;

Help me to be more obedient to Thy voice within me ;

Help me to serve Thee in some definite way ;

Help me to deny myself, and take up my cross daily, and follow Thee ;

I present myself a living sacrifice to Thee who hast died for me.

ii. Partaking of the Communion

When the communion day arrives, go to church in good time with an unhurried mind, and ask God to help you shut out all distracting thoughts, to give you a deep sense of the presence of Christ, and to bless the whole service to you and to others. Take part earnestly in the acts of worship that lead up to the communion. When the actual communion service begins, let your mind be filled with adoring thoughts of Him who, being God, yet became Man and dwelt among us, and died for our sins, and will one day be our Judge.

After praise and the reading of the words which record the institution of the sacrament, the minister will offer a prayer, in the course of which he will solemnly set apart the bread and wine for this holy use, and then the distribution will begin, and you will have a little time for quiet thought.

Remember the gracious invitation of Jesus : " Come unto Me, all ye that labour and are heavy laden, and I will give you rest. Take My yoke upon you and learn of Me ; for I am meek and lowly in heart ; and ye shall find rest unto your souls. For My yoke is easy and My burden is light."

Think how wonderful it is that God should forgive your sins—all your sins, even the worst; think how patient He is with you ; and thank Him very humbly that His mercy is greater than your sin. " Christ Jesus came into the world to save sinners, of whom I am chief."

Think how you are joining in an act of worship that unites you with Christians of all churches throughout the whole world, and with all the generations of believers who have passed away, and with the multitudes who will be followers of Jesus in centuries to come. What a fellowship it is ! " Ye are fellow-citizens with the saints, and of the household of God."

When the bread comes round, remember the words of Jesus : " Behold, I stand at the door and knock. If any man hear my voice and open the door, I will come in to him, and will sup with him, and he with Me." Say : " O Lord Jesus, I am listening now for Thy voice. I open the door of my heart to Thee. Come to me and sup with me, dear Lord, and be Thou every day the food of my soul."

When you take the cup of the covenant, say : " Lord Jesus, this Thy blood was shed for many for the remission of sins. Let my sins be forgiven, for Thy mercy's sake. Trusting in Thy strength I now put my sins away from me. Help me to live for Thee who didst die for me."

When you are waiting in the silence till all have partaken, do not look curiously about you, or fill your mind with idle thoughts. Be specially careful not to do anything to disturb the other worshippers. Think quietly what you can do or give up to make it more evident that you " have been with Jesus." Ask God to keep you, so that you may meet your Lord with joy, and not with shame and fear, at His appearing. Pray too for others that you may love and serve them better, and that you may all be true fellow-pilgrims on the heavenly way.

Do not be disappointed if you experience no profound stirring of your emotions, as if there were no blessing in the communion without this. If deep feeling does come be thankful ; but remember that the promise of the sacrament, the answer to your prayers, is not emotion, but Jesus Christ Himself. And He comes silently and secretly, and will make His presence felt in your life in a hundred quiet ways as the days go by.

CHAPTER V

THE LIFE OF COMMUNION

THE Lord's Supper is an act of communion with Christ, but it is also a reminder that *the whole life* of a Christian should be lived in communion with Him. That is the meaning of the words, " He that eateth My flesh and drinketh My Blood hath eternal life." This does not mean, " He that partakes of the Lord's Supper," but, " He that makes Jesus Christ his life—as it were his daily food."

We cannot be true disciples of Christ without taking pains about our inner life. It is not by our own strength that we shall become good men and women, but only by His Spirit dwelling in us. Our task is to keep in contact with Him : " Abide in Me, and I in you. As the branch cannot bear fruit of itself except it abide in the vine, so neither can ye, except ye abide in Me. I am the vine, ye are the branches." How then are we to " abide in Christ " ?

i. Use the Means of Grace

When our fathers spoke of " the means of grace " they meant the divine helps to a good life. What are they ?

1. *Prayer.*

This is the almost instinctive way of drawing near to God. There can be no real religion without prayer. We *must* find time each day for a few minutes' talk with God— about our sins and our duties, our trials, our friends, and our Saviour. We ought certainly to *begin and end* each day with Him, but we should accustom ourselves also to speak to Him at other times, even in the midst of our work. We can send out a silent cry for help at any time, and it is never in vain. No matter how much in earnest you may be at present, you will quickly grow cold and hard unless you pray.

2. *Devotional reading.*

We need not only to speak to God, but to let Him speak to us, and we never hear His voice so clearly as when, seeking His guidance, we read some portions of the Bible. We ought to read it devotionally, not merely to become familiar with its narratives or its poetry, but to " hear what God the Lord will speak " to our hearts and consciences. For this purpose certain portions of Scripture are peculiarly valuable—the Gospels, for example, parts of the Epistles, many of the Psalms. There are some little books of selections, like *Daily Light,* which many have found useful ; and the reading of a brief " meditation " may help to recall us to the realities we are so apt to forget. But we should train ourselves to read, each day, something that will bring us near to God. We need to take pains to keep *any* friendship in repair, and it is only through prayer and carefully-chosen devotional reading that we are enabled to keep in repair this highest of all friendships.*

3. *The Fellowship of the Church.*

The principal observance that holds the members of the Church together is the meeting for public worship. The Christian life is not individual alone, but social. *We need one another*—in worship as in other things. It is fellowship in Church life with its regular worship, its sacraments, its preaching of the Word, and its varied opportunities of service, that keeps alive our sense of brotherhood in Christ. You will be a very stunted sort of Christian unless you share in the rich, full life of a congregation. " Where two or three are

* There are many helps to prayer, such as William Barclay's *The Plain Man's Book of Prayers* and *Prayers for Young People;* and in the meditations and prayers in the Daily Readings of the Bible Reading Fellowship, the International Bible Reading Association and the Scripture Union.

gathered together in My Name, there am I in the midst of them."

4. *The Lord's Day.*

From the very beginning the Church has kept sacred the day on which Christ rose from the dead. In heathen countries one of the distinctive marks of a Christian is that he keeps Sunday. If it were wholly, or even very largely, given over to work and pleasure, there would be little opportunity for united worship, for the religious training of young people, for the carrying on of evangelistic work. The Christian Sunday is one of the most precious " means of grace " we have. Use it then for the highest ends. How would Christ like you to spend the day which brings so wonderful an opportunity for seeking Him and doing something for Him ?

This is not the place to discuss what you may do or not do on Sunday. How you spend it will be a test of your real loyalty to your Master and His cause. It is not by doing on Sundays what may be innocently done on other days that we chiefly sin against the sacredness of the Lord's Day, but by *not doing* what would help us to be more spiritually minded and unselfish followers of Christ.

Be methodical.

In connection with all these " means of grace " we need to make rules for ourselves. We soon grow slack if we just pray when we feel inclined, or read the Bible when we have a minute or two to spare from our amusements, or go to church it it happens to suit our mood. We cannot afford to leave our spiritual life to the mercy of chance or impulse. It needs discipline. We should observe set times for prayer and devotional reading, and attend church as a matter of course. You will be no good servant of Christ if you do not learn to deny yourself many harmless liberties for His sake.

ii. Guard the Honour of Christ

Remember that our Lord commits His honour to those who profess to be His. You know how you have been shocked to see among the professed disciples of Christ some whose lives have " put Him to open shame." Nothing in the world so hinders His cause as the inconsistencies of His followers. And now *you* are to be numbered among those who have entered into covenant with Him. You cannot possibly remain in true communion with Christ and allow yourself anything you know to be wrong. " The cup of blessing which we bless, is it not the communion of the blood of Christ ? . . . Ye cannot drink the cup of the Lord AND the cup of devils." May God keep you from falling away from Him.

It was a dreadful thing for Peter when, after he had denied Jesus, the high priest's servant said to him, " Did not I see thee in the garden with Him ? " Take care that no one has ever occasion to say to you, in surprise or pain or mockery, " But—did not I see you at communion with Him ? " Try rather, by the beauty of your life—by your sensitive avoidance of evil, and your cheerful and loving service of your fellows—to win others to think well of Christ and His Church.

iii. Trust the Promises of Christ

You are not setting out on the Christian life alone or unaided. The whole power of God is on the side of those that look to Him for help ; He will " strengthen you with might by His Spirit." Christ is " able to save to the uttermost them that come unto God by Him, seeing He ever liveth to make intercession for them."

" My grace is sufficient for thee, for My strength is made perfect in weakness."

" I KNOW WHOM I HAVE BELIEVED, AND AM PERSUADED THAT HE IS ABLE TO KEEP THAT WHICH I HAVE COMMITTED UNTO HIM, AGAINST THAT DAY."

PRINTED IN GREAT BRITAIN BY
BELL, AIRD & COGHILL LTD., GLASGOW